About the Author

Jane Begley lives near the sea which she loves and spends a lot of time exploring the coast nearby. Her garden is another source of delight.

She started writing two years ago after meeting a man who touched her heart and soul.

She has two children and five lovely grandchildren.

This book is dedicated to the man who touched my heart and soul and inspired me to write.

Jane Begley

THE BEAUTY OF LIFE

Copyright © Jane Begley (2015)

The right of Jane Begley to be identified as author of this work has been asserted by her in accordance with section 77 and 78 of the Copyright, Designs and Patents Act 1988.

All rights reserved. No part of this publication may be reproduced, stored in a retrieval system, or transmitted in any form or by any means, electronic, mechanical, photocopying, recording, or otherwise, without the prior permission of the publishers.

Any person who commits any unauthorized act in relation to this publication may be liable to criminal prosecution and civil claims for damages.

A CIP catalogue record for this title is available from the British Library.

ISBN 978 178455 105 6

www.austinmacauley.com

First Published (2015)
Austin Macauley Publishers Ltd.
25 Canada Square
Canary Wharf
London
E14 5LB

Printed and bound in Great Britain

The Beauty of Life

Beauty is in the love of two people for each other
Beauty is in the rose and its wondrous smell
Beauty is in the sky and its changing colours and movement
Beauty is in the simplicity of life when all is well

There is no beauty without love
There is no beauty without awareness
There is no beauty if you cannot feel and sense what is in your heart
There is no beauty if you cannot share this beauty with another

When all is well life can be beautiful
When all is well life can be enjoyed
When all is well we can see, sense and feel the beauty around us
When all is well beauty is in the simplicity of life

Support

We all need support at some stage in our lives
We all need the support of another
We all need to feel we can confide in another
We need the love of another

Being alone is not what we want
Being alone is not what we need
We need to share our feelings with another
We need to share our thoughts with another

We cannot be happy when we are alone
When there is no one to share with
When there is no one to tell our troubles to
When there is no one to share our thoughts

We need the support of another
We need the love of another
We need to share our life with another
Without support of another it is no life at all

Along The Coast

As I walk along the coast I sigh
Breathing in the fresh air and the salty smell of the sea
Feeling free as a bird I stride out along the path
The sun is out and the sea is a deep deep blue
The wind is warm on my face

No one in sight I feel like the only person in the world
The only person to witness this breath-taking sight
The only person to feel such calm and serenity
No one in sight just the gulls soaring on the wind
And the sun beating down on my face

As I round the bend I notice a tiny wren flitting here and there
And the brown bracken is looking a bit worse for wear
The wind picks up and the gulls soar even higher
I stop a while and gaze at the sea as it sparkles in the sun
What pleasure can be had from walking along the coast

Dreams

I sit by the sea and dream of you
I sit by the sea and think of you

I listen to the gulls out to sea
I listen to the waves as they lap the shore

I imagine a life that's full of love
I imagine a life that's happy and full

I feel the soft gentle breeze as it caresses my face
I feel the soft sand between my toes

I see myself swimming in the deep blue sea
I see you there along side of me
Happy dreams and happy times to come

Above Us

Above us is only sky or so it seems
All around us is only sky or so it seems
What else is above us
Awareness is above us
Above us and around us is awareness
Awareness of life and awareness of feelings
Awareness of beauty and awareness of space

Are we aware of people's feelings
Are we aware of the space around us
Are we aware of the beauty in life
Without love there is no awareness
Without love we are not aware of people's feelings
We are not aware of space
We are not aware of the beauty of life
We are not aware of what is above us and around us

Special

What makes us special
What makes us different

A special person is a person who cares
A special person is a person who can feel love

A special person is connected to themselves
A special person is connected to love

A special person is aware of others
A special person is touched by love

If you are aware of everything around you
You are special indeed

My garden

When life gets me down and things don't go right
My garden is my refuge and I attack it with might
I cut down hedges and shrubs that have gone wild
I move things around and plant lots of new

I forget about life and all its pitfalls
I just concentrate on putting the garden to rights
I plant it with roses and plants galore
I dig out weeds and change things around

When spring comes around and the bulbs all appear
I marvel at how they all just appear
Roses are my special delight and I fill every space with more and more
My garden is large and can always take more

Cutting the grass is another delight
And the pleasure I get from the after effect
When summer comes around it is filled with scent
What pleasure can be had from things going wrong

Heaven

They say heaven is where the good go
What is this place called heaven
Is heaven a place where everything is perfect
Is heaven a place where all our troubles disappear
Is heaven the only place where everything is perfect

Is it possible to have heaven on earth
Is it possible for everything to be perfect here on earth
What is perfect anyway, is perfect for one person the same as perfect for another
Is heaven for one person the same as heaven for another
Perhaps one day we shall find out

Joined

Nothing can compare to a rose on a summers day
The smell of a new mown lawn
The sound and the smell of the sea as it rushes to the shore
The sight of a swallow as it swoops and dives catching flies

Can anything compare to watching the sun as it rises on the horizon
Or to watching the sun set across the sea
To the sound of an owl hooting in the dead of night
Or the sound of a blackbird guarding its nest

The only thing that can compare to all of these
Is the love between two people as they come together as one
The joy as they enjoy these sights and smells together
And the love that joins all these things together

Beyond

What is beyond this life on earth
Is there a life beyond this life on earth
Where is it that our spirit comes from and goes to
Is there another world beyond this one
Is there perhaps somewhere else we cannot see
Somewhere else invisible to the human eye

If there is such a place is it somewhere on another planet
Is it somewhere outside of this space
Is it somewhere never to be seen by the naked eye
Perhaps it is in another dimension
Another world entirely that can be neither seen or even imagined
Let us hope that this world is a peaceful and loving place

Colours

Life would be drab indeed without colour
Colour is part of who we are
Colour is everywhere
Colour is in the words that we speak

I marvel at the colours on the grass as the sun beats down
At the blues in the sky as the clouds move across
When the sun is out everything is clear and bright
When the sun disappears a change comes about

What a spectacular sight is a field full of golden corn
Or a rose in bloom
The rain pores down and suddenly a rainbow appears
Brightening the day

But the colour best of all is the colour of words
Words on a page that touch the heart
Words of love and kindness
Words of hope and appreciation

Today

There is a hint of magic in the air
A hint that spring is not far away
Already the blackbirds are looking for a mate
And the blue tits are searching for a nest

The clouds all fluffy and white
Are moving swiftly along the horizon
The sky although blue is just a little too pale
But all around everything appears bright

There is a feeling of expectation in the air
A feeling that life is about to show itself
That buds will start to appear
And birds will start to sing

Hooray for the changing seasons
The feeling that life is never the same
And you can never be absolutely sure
What it will bring from day to day

Touched

Touch can be a powerful thing
Without touch a baby will not live
Without touch we wilt and die

Without touch the heart will slowly give up
Without touch the soul cannot survive
Touch can be a powerful thing

Touch is an expression of love
Touch is a feeling expressed
Without touch we cannot express love
Touch is a powerful thing

Angels

Angels we are led to believe are powerful beings
Angels we are led to believe are only seen by the few
Do angels exist or are they only a figment of our imagination
Perhaps there are Angels in disguise in different parts of the world
Perhaps one day they will be revealed for all to see
Perhaps one day we will all become angels in disguise
One day when the world changes
One day when humans decide to live side by side
One day when peace reigns we will all be Angels

The Soul

Our soul is deep inside us
Our soul is the essence of who we are
It is our soul that guides us through life
If we do not listen to our soul
We can never be happy

Our soul speaks to us through our feelings
Our soul speaks to us through our heart
If we do not listen to our feelings
If we do not listen to our heart
Our soul will wilt and die

Do not be discouraged when things go wrong
Do not be discouraged when you become stuck
Our soul is strong and powerful
Just wait a while until things feel right
Then your soul will guide you on

Energy

Energy is within us
Energy is around us and below us
Energy is felt but unseen

Without energy we could not live
Without energy we could not move
Without energy we could not touch

Energy moves around us and within us
Without love we have no energy
Without energy we have no love

Living Life to the Full

There are many ways of living life to the full
Life can be lived to the full without any happiness
Life can be lived to the full without feeling anything

Life can only truly be lived to the full if it is enjoyed
Life can only really be lived to the full if it is shared
Life without love is not life at all

Most of us go through life feeling there should be more
Most of us go through life feeling discontent and frustrated
Most of us go through life not even being aware of it

What is it that we are all looking for
What is it that would make us happy
What else but love

Feeling Good

When I walk by the sea I feel good
When the sun shines I feel good
When I loiter in the garden I feel good

I go for a brisk long walk and I feel good
I dig over my garden and I feel good
I listen to the birds sing and I feel good

When I have a good clear out I feel good
When I clean my house I feel good
When I wear something new I feel good

When I have a good stretch I feel good
When I sit on the sofa and watch a good film
When I make a cup of tea at the end of the day
When I lie with my lover and contemplate the day

Beneath Us

Beneath us is the earth
Beneath us is the soul of the earth
Beneath us the earth lives and breathes

Beneath us there are unknown and untapped elements
Beneath us the earth pulses and breathes
When the earth is angry it vents its feelings on the earth above

Above the earth we feel the wrath of the earth beneath
Above the earth we feel the changing soul beneath
When the earth is angry it must show its feelings to the earth above

The earth is a powerful planet it has hidden depth and hidden energy
Above the earth its energy connects with the sun and the moon
Below the earth it connects with the energy of its soul

The earth is a powerful planet indeed

Coming Together

Nothing can compare to two people coming together as one
Nothing can compare to two people in love
Nothing can compare to two people in love sharing their life together

When two people come together as one they are totally in tune with each other
When two people come together as one their souls unite as one
When two people come together as one their hearts are touched

When two people who are meant to be together are united as one
They cannot be torn apart, they cannot be separated
Their hearts and souls unite as one

Hurt

There are so many ways to be hurt
There are so many ways to feel hurt
Hurt comes from inside
Hurt can come from outside when it is physical
Hurt from inside can be deep or it can be light

When we are hurt it touches our heart and our soul
Hurt can make us angry and hurt can make us sad
Hurt can reach right down into our soul and linger for a lifetime
If we do not recognise this hurt it can affect our lives
If we do not share this hurt it will not go away

Do not let this hurt destroy your life
Do not let this hurt affect your life
Hurt is just a feeling to be expressed
Hurt can be healed by love
When we are hurt we need love
Hurt is a powerful feeling

By The Sea

Walking by the sea a feeling of calm comes over me
I breathe in the clean salty air and relax
Looking out towards the horizon the sea appears endless
There is a strong breeze and the sea is choppy
The sun suddenly shows itself and transforms the world around
The sea turns a dark blue out to sea and turquoise towards the shore
A smooth rock suddenly seems inviting and I sit down
Shading my eyes from the glare of the sun I watch the children as they play
Buckets and spades digging in the sand full of wonder and delight
They rush down to the water's edge shouting to each other
Jumping over waves, clothes getting soaking wet
I turn my head towards the rocks where mums and dads alike
With fishing nets and buckets at the ready spend hour upon hour
With their offspring searching for crabs and shrimps and tiny fish
What better way to spend a day than down by the sea

Flowers

There is a beauty in flowers that can never be compared
Wherever you are in the world there are always flowers
Flowers of every conceivable colour
Flowers of every conceivable shape
There are flowers on the ground
Flowers on the shrubs and flowers on the trees
There are even flowers in the desert and flowers in the snow
There are flowers that have amazing smells from sweet to sour
And carpets of flowers that dazzle your eyes
What beauty can be seen anywhere in the world

Frost

I step out one early frosty morning
I feel the crunch of the frost beneath my feet
Everywhere is white
The sun comes up and the frost sparkles

The air is cold as I climb over the stile
I feel the sun touch my face as it slowly rises
The air is clean and fresh
The sound of birds singing is all around

I stride out quickly in the cold air
And take the path towards the sea
A blackbird appears chasing his mate
A sign that spring is just around the corner

When I reach the sea all is calm
The sun rises higher in the sky
The seagulls are screeching up above
What a joy it is to be up and about so early on a frosty
morning

Birds

As spring approaches and the air is fresh and sweet
The air becomes alive with the sound of birds singing
The sight of a blackbird chasing after a mate
And the beauty of the blue tit searching for a nest

Have you ever stopped to wonder at the amazing sight
And the clear bright colours of a woodpecker tapping at a tree
When you look up to the sky you may even spy
A hawk hovering in one spot or a buzzard riding the thermals

What better sight or delight than a swan in full flight
Have you ever seen a tiny wren scampering around
In and out, up and down searching for food
With its turned up tail bobbing this way and that

The magical sight of the shy speckled thrush
Working so hard to open a snail
Or the dainty coloured blue tit
Endlessly searching for insects to feed her young

When the swallows and house martins appear
You know that summer is on the way
And if you are lucky enough to see their nests
You will marvel at such an amazing sight

You may gaze in awe if you spot the starlings
As they swoop and dive at the end of the day
As they make their way back home to roost
What amazing sights are to be had just by seeing what is about

Calm

How calm is the sea today
How calm and still is the air
The seagulls are high catching the thermals
And water flows gently downstream calming the soul

The sun is out warming my heart
And shining down upon the sea
Shadows appear across the path
And birds are busy everywhere

Out to sea a lonely sailing boat
And the Mewstone stands alone
Down the track I go with not a soul in sight
And a kestrel hovers overhead

Close to the shore the sea is a turquoise blue
While out to sea it's a deep dark blue
The sun shines down and warms my face
And all is right with the world

Hope

Hope is what keeps us going
Hope for a better time to come
Faith in life, a life still to come
Faith that love will see us through

When all else fails and nothing seems clear
We listen to our hearts to see us through
We do what feels right and trust in life
And that all will come together at just the right time

Hope for love and hope for a better life
Hope for peace and hope for fun and laughter
Without love or without fun, life cannot go on
For the spirit will falter and eventually die

So lift up you heart and see what's inside
And trust in life to see you through
For life has a habit of coming together
Coming together at just the right time

At Last

At last we meet again
At last I touch and feel you
I feel your skin next to mine
I feel you deep inside me

It seems like we have never been apart
It feels like we have never been apart
It feels so good to touch you
So good to know you are lying next to me

The months seem to melt away
And it seems like they never were
Just for those few hours
All the waiting has been worth it

Until we meet again my love

The World As We Know It

How many of us stop to think of the world we live in
Stop to wonder how it can exist as it does
The only living planet in the universe

Do we ever wonder why
Do we ever see the beauty in it
Do we look at ourselves and wonder how we came here

Do we ever wonder if there is a special reason for us being here
A reason that we came here
Perhaps there is something in particular that we are meant to be doing
Are we perhaps drawn to particular people or particular places

Is there something that gives us energy and enthusiasm
Are we even aware of what is around us
Do we look at the world and think what an amazing place it is
Or do we just go through life with blinkers on

The world we live in is a very special place
The world we live in is unique and filled with beauty
The world we live in needs to be loved and nurtured
Just as we all need to be loved and nurtured

Above and Below

Above the earth are millions of planets
And a space which seems to go on for eternity
Is there a place where it eventually stops
What is the purpose of this never ending space

Is there perhaps another world
A world just like ours
A world that we could never reach
Perhaps it is a place where the people are more advanced

A place that can be reached only when we die
A place where we can see where we have gone wrong
A place where we have a chance to make amends
A place where we are given a second chance

If there is such a place
If we do get a second chance
Perhaps next time we will be happier
Perhaps we will remember why we are here

Perhaps we will look around us and see what a beautiful place
this is

Around the World

No one can deny the world is full of beauty and delight
That there are never two days exactly alike
That there are never two countries exactly the same

What wonders can be seen that take your breath away
What experiences can be had if you take a look around
How the scenery can change from desert to mountain top

From Alaska to Africa the world couldn't be much different
From Great Britain to Canada is quaint villages to open plains
How can you compare Tahiti to a cold winter in Russia

When you travel South you could hit Cape Town
When you go North, Greenland you will behold
Travel to the East and down a bit, China you will reach

If you fancy a trip to the West you could tour around the United States
If you go right round to the other side you could take a holiday in Fiji or Hawaii
If it's a mainland that you prefer then try New Zealand or Sydney in Australia

Wherever the fancy takes you there are wonders to behold
Whether you like to bask in the sun or swim in the ocean
Whether you prefer to climb a mountain or go on safari
The world is full of such wondrous places

The Nature of Love

Love is a wondrous feeling
A feeling that goes deep into the soul

Love gives us hope and understanding
Understanding of life and our surroundings

Love can fulfil our dreams
Dreams of fulfilment and purpose

Love brings us closer to nature
Nature brings us closer to our soul

Our soul is the core of our being
Our being is where we belong

We belong where we feel is right
Right is where we belong

We belong where we are loved

Forever Yours

Love comes at unexpected times
It sometimes begins slowly and grows
And it sometimes somersaults into being
It sometimes fizzles out with time
And it sometimes, very rarely, never dies

Love that comes so rarely must be nourished
Love that comes so rarely must be honoured
Love like this should never be ignored
It comes but once in a lifetime
And is honest and true

Nature

What would we do if we couldn't see the sun rise
If there were no rain to make the plants and flowers grow
If there were no birds flying in the sky
If there were no trees silhouetted on the horizon

What if we couldn't smell the freshly cut grass
Or smell the honeysuckle on a balmy evening
If we couldn't enjoy the fresh salty smell of the sea
Or the smell of a bright sunny day in May

What would we do if we could never experience
The amazing feeling of swimming in the sea
Or we could never climb a hill and breathe in
The freshness and feel the exhilaration in our body

What if we could never feel the love between two people
Or experience the ultimate pleasure of making love
This is a world full of wonder and delight
This is a world that should never be ignored

The Sea

How would we live without the sea
A world beyond compare
From the deep dark depths of the oceans
To the calm of the lapping tide as it finds the shore

Beneath the depth of the ocean
Is a world beyond belief
With fish the colours of a rainbow
And plants of a peculiar nature

From the tiniest micro-organisms
To the giant creatures of the deep
The world that lives beneath the sea
Is a world beyond belief

Many a fisherman's tale is told
About the giant creatures of the sea
From giant octopus to whales as big as a ship
But the greatest tale of all is about the beauty of the deep

The changing face of the sea can be as different as they come
From calm and still as can be to a wall so powerful and high
It can destroy a whole town or country
Many a ship or island has been lost to the sea

The sea holds many secrets
Secrets that should never be known
For the power and might of the sea
Has an energy and a soul of its own

Flowers of the World

The rose has a beauty all of its own
A beauty that you just want to touch and smell
From the softest of pink to the warmth of apricot
Such amazing colours of every hue

When you walk through the woods
In spring or early June
You will be amazed to find a carpet of blue
Tiny bells clustered together with a smell so divine

You may even find a primrose or two
Whose soft shades of yellow can touch the heart
Later on in the year the foxgloves appear
Whose soft shades of pink will make you blink

In each and every season there are flowers to be seen
In meadows and gardens and even by the sea
When winter seems never to end
Suddenly snowdrops push their way through the ground

The delicate white bells of the snowdrops
Followed by the bright sunshine yellow of the daffodils
Give us hope when we are feeling down
And let us know that spring is soon to be found

When the bright reds and yellows of the tulips appear
You know spring is well underway
It won't be too long before the rose buds you see
And butterflies follow soon after

When the sun warms the ground the plants come alive
The world is transformed to all shades of green
Plants that are meant to climb towards the sun
And everywhere you look such beauty you will see

Purples and reds, pinks and blues, colours of every shade
When the sun is out to brighten up the day
Such colours can dazzle your senses
With each passing day a new flower appears
Opening your heart and lifting your spirits
What would we do without flowers

The Sky

The sky is filled with wonder and delight
It changes every minute of every day
It changes with the wind
It changes with the seasons
And it changes with the tides

One minute it is cloudy and dull
And the next blue, sunny and bright
Clouds appear of every imaginable shape
Gliding across the sky with pure delight

It can brighten the day or dampen the spirit
It is never ending and never beginning
One minute it is as dark as thunder
The next as blue as can be

Looking one way the clouds are moving east
Looking in the opposite direction and they appear to move west
Sunny and bright to the west, cloudy and dull to the east
Raining in one direction, bright and blue in the other

One day it appears a million miles high
And the next, clouds are hanging close to the ground
Torrential rain and bright and sunny
All in the same day

When winter is upon us and the sky looks dark and heavy
The sky opens up and the snow descends upon us
Covering the land with a carpet of white
Dazzling our senses and filling us with awe

At the break of dawn when the sun appears
And night turns to day
The light in the sky has a magical glow
Welcoming the start of a brand new day

When day turns to night and the sun goes down
The colours of the sky can amaze us all
From purple to pink and from orange to red
The sun setting in the sky is an absolute delight

The sky is full of amazing sights
From the colours in a rainbow
To the darkest of nights
Filled with a million shining stars
And the light from a brilliant full moon

How often we can gaze in wonder
Just by looking at the sky

Needs

Love and friendship are needs in everyone's life
A need to be loved and a need to be heard

Happiness is something we all search for and need
Without happiness we will not survive

To be happy with the way we are
And to be happy with the way we feel and look

These needs are simple and basic
But without them our spirit cannot survive

We all need fresh air to breathe
And we all need exercise for our body to feel good

In order to feel good about ourselves we need all of these
But to feel happy and content we need love most of all

The Horizon

There is much more on the horizon than you can ever imagine
Life has so much in store for all of us
Around each corner there is a new horizon
A new part of our lives that we are unaware of
A new chapter yet to be discovered
When one chapter ends there is always another
One that could be much better than the last

We all of us have more than one chapter in our lives
But we all have an ultimate goal
A goal that is really quite simple
That goal is to find ourselves and to find love
To find happiness and to find contentment
If we fail to find love and ourselves
Our spirit will start to give up and we grow old too soon
So never give up looking for love and your spirit will carry you through

Love Is All There Is

Love comes from the heart
Love comes from within
Love is contagious
Love makes the world go round

Without love there is nothing to live for
Without love you cannot see the beauty in life
Without love you cannot feel what is in your heart
Without love you are not connected to yourself

If you have never been touched by love
If you have never experienced love
You cannot be the person you are meant to be
Love is the most powerful feeling there is

Walking Along the Lane Today

Walking along the lane today I notice how pretty the
hedgerows are looking
Bluebells and pink campions are in abundance now
With bright yellow buttercups dotted here and there
Everywhere is fresh and green brightening up even a cloudy
day

As I get to the estuary I stop and admire the view
In a field nearby, brown cows are contemplating the day
And the yachts are bobbing about on the tide
Out to see the view of the Mewstone is always good to see

I continue along the path towards the point and notice
How bright the gorse is with its shiny yellow flowers
The sea is choppy today and rather grey like the day
I continue my walk along the path with the ponies grazing
nearby

I am feeling rather sad today and rather lonely too
For however lovely the countryside is and however nice the
walk
It is never the same if you have no one to share it with
No one to enjoy it with and no one to love you by your side…

What If

We could have whatever we wanted
What would we choose
Would we choose to be rich and famous
Would we choose to live in a big house
Or would we choose love

Would we be happy living in a big house without love
Would we be happy with lots of money without love
Would we enjoy being famous without love
Without love we can never be happy
How nice it would be however if
We could have all of these things and love

Trees

They spread their branches
They shed their leaves
They protect us from the rays of the sun
Without them our world would die

They give us fuel for the fire
They give us paper and things to make
They provide us with food to eat
They are a source of wonder in every way

In winter they are bare
But their beauty is beyond compare
If you look towards the horizon
You will see their silhouette against the sky

In spring a change comes about
And their shoots begin to appear
Their leaves start to unfold
And on some catkins will appear

The sun warms their roots and leaves
And they gradually come alive
With leaves of amazing shapes and sizes
And flowers beyond belief

When the chill of autumn starts to set in
Their leaves begin to change again
Amazing colours of reds and browns
Adorn the sky and cover the ground
What would we do without the trees
What sort of life would come about
A life that would not be long
As life would be extinct without the trees

On a Wing and a Prayer

If I had my life over again
If I could change just one thing
If I could make just one wish
I would be with you now

I would live my life forever in your company
I would be the mother of your children
I would make love to you every day
I would comfort you and hold you

Life is for living with love
Life is precious and so are you

The Power of Love

Love has a power all of its own
A power that can surprise us all
When it touches the heart
When it touches the soul
It can consume us all

When it is honest and true
It can help us through
Even the darkest of times
It can keep us going
Even though we would give up

A heart that is loved
A heart that is true
Will pull us through
And not let us give up
Will not let us die

Love has a power that is untouchable